The Shark

Silent Hunter

text by Renée le Bloas and Jérôme Julienne
photos by the BIOS Agency

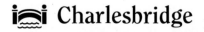 Charlesbridge

Library of Congress Cataloging-in-Publication Data
le Bloas, Renée and Julienne, Jérôme
   [le requin, tueur silencieux. English]
The Shark: Silent Hunter/text by Renée le Bloas and Jérôme
Julienne. photographs by the BIOS agency.
     p.   cm. — (Animal close-ups)
   Summary: Describes the physical characteristics, hunting
techniques, reproduction, reputation, and some different species
of sharks.
ISBN 0-88106-258-8 (softcover)
   1. Sharks—Juvenile literature. [1. Sharks.] I. Julienne,
Jérôme. II. Title. III. Series.
QL638.9.L39 1998   97-43254
597.3—dc21

Copyright © 1997 by Éditions Milan under the title *le requin, tueur silencieux*
300, rue Léon-Joulin, 31101 Toulouse Cedex 100, France
French series editor, Valérie Tracqui
Translated by Cambridge Translation Resources
Additional research by Jane Reynolds

Copyright © 1998 by Charlesbridge Publishing
Published by Charlesbridge Publishing, 85 Main Street, Watertown, MA 02472 • (617) 926-0329
www.charlesbridge.com
Printed in Korea
10 9 8 7 6 5 4

The gray reef shark grows up to seven feet long. It usually swims close to the bottom, but may come to the surface to search for prey.

Shark!

A coral reef looks like a garden. Multicolored fish swirl in the blue water or nibble at the coral with their parrot-like beaks. At the opening of its hole, a moray eel sways with the current. Hungry crabs crack little shellfish between their claws. The reef bustles with activity.

Suddenly a fin breaks the surface. A dark shadow glides above the coral. It's the gray reef shark on the prowl for easy prey—the weak or the injured. The grouper hide, watching this quiet killer out of the corners of their eyes.

The hunter continues its silent swim. Slowly, its shadow disappears into the deep blue. . . .

These sharks live in the warm waters of the tropics. They live in coral reefs, along the reef wall, or in sand channels and lagoons.

Living torpedo

Built for speed, the gray reef shark's tapered body slides smoothly through the water. From above, its dark back blends with the black of the depths, and seen from below, its white belly is lost in the light of the surface. Its powerful tail is its propeller and the pectoral fins, on its side, direct it up or down. The broad rigid fins on top of its body—the dorsal fins—keep its body upright in the water. It can accelerate with lightning speed, and reach up to twenty-five miles per hour.

Its extremely flexible skeleton, unlike that of bony fish, is made entirely of cartilage. The oil that fills its enormous liver allows it to float effortlessly at any depth.

In the past, the shark's streamlined form inspired the design of submarines and planes.

A remora attaches itself to the shark with a suction cup. This little fish eats the parasites that infest the shark's skin.

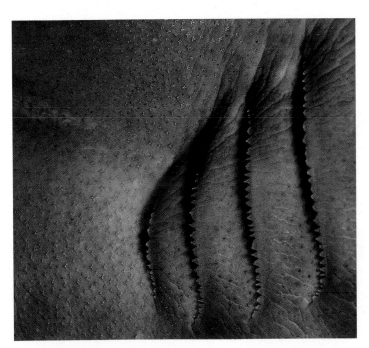

The shark has no scales like fish have. Its rough skin is covered with thousands of tiny teeth called denticles.

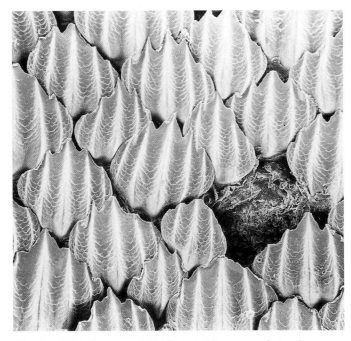

The denticles form grooves that guide water along the shark's body without making ripples.

The size of the gray reef shark's territory depends on how deep the water is and how much food there is.

The tiger shark attacks rays, sea birds, other sharks, and sometimes even humans.

The gray reef shark may attack when threatened. But first it faces its enemy with its mouth half open, lowers its fins, and arches its back.

To each his own!

Each gray reef shark has its own territory. Within it, it always follows the same routes and only allows sharks smaller than itself to enter.

A dreaded tiger shark swims into its territory. This sixteen-foot giant is one of the most dangerous sharks. It has left the open sea to hunt for fish on the reef.

The gray reef shark tries to intimidate the intruder with a strange underwater dance. It spins around, arches its back, raises its snout, and lowers its fins. The message is: "Get out of my territory!" If the intruder keeps coming, the reef shark will attack, at the risk of being eaten.

This time, the uninvited guest goes on its way.

Round up!

A school of a hundred pompano passes in the distance. The fish and their grunts create a slight movement in the water, which the shark senses and hears. It gets excited, and its agitation spreads along the reef like a shock wave. In a few minutes, the gray reef sharks assemble. One, two, three, ten, thirty— they come from everywhere. They fly through the water like torpedoes.

Nervous, they brush against each other. To avoid bloody battles, they spread out, swimming side by side. There is no leader—the smaller sharks make way for the bigger ones.

They advance in a tight formation like a squadron of fighter jets.

Gray reef sharks may gather to hunt in packs of fifty or more.

Special cells on the sides of the shark's body detect movement in the water.

Sensors on the snout detect the electrical fields made by living things.

The shark's nostrils are not for breathing—only for smelling.

Sharks and rays are the only fish with electrical sensors called ampullae of Lorenzini. They detect prey without seeing it, hearing it, or sensing its movements.

On the hunt

The sharks track the school of fish. All their senses are alert. They listen with their whole bodies. Hundreds of tiny sensors along their bodies can feel the slightest movement in the water.

If one of the fish is bleeding, the sharks can trace the trail of the odor quickly. They sway their heads left and right and follow the side that smells the odor most strongly.

Once the prey is in view, the sharks hunt by sight. They see very well, in color. One of them goes after the wounded fish. When it gets nearer, it feels the electrical waves given off by the prey with the special sensors on its snout. This sixth sense tells it the fish is exhausted. It can attack.

Fresh teeth

The shark is cautious. It swims around its prey for a long time to examine it closely. To smell the fish better, the shark bumps it with its snout and returns to careful circling. Suddenly, it bites the fish and lets it go. The pompano tastes good.

At last the hungry shark pulls its snout up and opens its enormous mouth. Its razor-sharp teeth close on the catch. Then it shakes its head violently back and forth. The fish is cut clean in two.

The shark has several rows of razor-sharp teeth.

When a tooth falls out, one from the next row slides in to take its place in just a few days. This impressive weapon never wears out.

Sharks can go days without eating anything. But when they do eat, they stuff themselves. This school of pompano is a swimming feast.

The sharks scan the reef. Thanks to the electrical sensors in their snouts, they easily locate all prey hiding there.

During the attack the shark may lose a few teeth, but new ones move in very quickly. Pilot fish feast on the scraps.

Gray reef sharks are not picky. They eat pompano, small grouper, snapper— all the bony fish of the reef. They also eat squid, octopus, lobster, and crab. Like wolves, sharks prefer wounded or sick animals, which are easier to catch, but will take on a large fish if it is caught on a line or injured.

In a "feeding frenzy," gray reef sharks fight over some bait. But this fury is actually a dance with strict rules. They bite each other only by accident.

A dance of death

Sharks play the feeding game according to the rules. The biggest always go first, and each one takes its turn.

The feast complete, a shark swims lazily away. The fish nearby now have nothing to fear.

Recently killed, an enormous fish, weighing more than two hundred pounds, floats on the surface. Attracted by the smell of blood, the sharks approach. They quickly act —no circling this time. The abundance of food, their excitement, and the blood make them lose control.

A shark suddenly sinks its teeth into the bait. Now the feeding frenzy begins. The sharks all pounce on the fish, taking huge bites with their jaws. With a muffled sound, bones crack between their teeth. The water grows cloudy with sand, blood, and scraps of food.

Finally, the last mouthful is gulped down. Then in an instant, the sea grows calm. The sharks swim off peacefully.

Shark babies

One year after mating, the mother-to-be leaves the reef for the shelter of a lagoon to give birth. She lays down on the sand in shallow water. Soon the baby sharks come into the world. But the mother does not take care of them. They are just strangers she might want to eat. So the mother's body makes a substance that dulls her appetite. She won't want to eat anything for several days.

The little sharks, left on their own, hunt for prey their own size: shrimp, little fish. They grow up in a miniature troop in the lagoon.

Seven years later, now adults, they will return to the reef's wall. They live there for twenty-five years.

Researchers place tiny transmitters under the skin of a baby shark to track its movements as it grows up. They also put a plastic tag on the mother shark's fin to identify it in case a sport fisher catches it.

Some sharks give birth to live offspring. They may have one baby or as many as three hundred, depending on the species.

Other sharks produce eggs. In some species, the eggs hatch inside the mother's body. The baby feeds on the reserves of the egg.

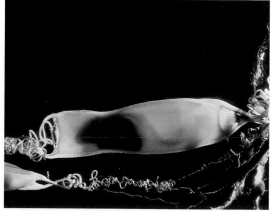

The dogfish lays its eggs in a very sturdy casing in the water.

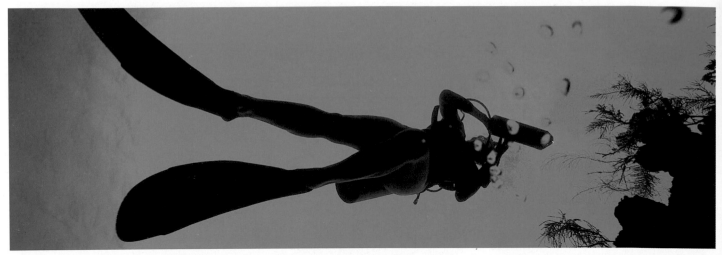

Sharks can pick the wrong target when looking into the sunlight. They may mistake a diver for a seal or a sea turtle, then let him go.

A shark fin should not inspire so much fear.

To watch a shark, stay motionless with arms close to the body. A bite from a shark, even a small one, can be serious.

Face-to-face

On the reef, a diver marvels at the sight of the coral. He doesn't know he's just entered the territory of a gray reef shark.

The shark approaches. Not to eat him—its hunter's instinct draws it to its most familiar prey. But it is curious. The shark swims around the diver at a distance. Many swimmers have been "sniffed out" by sharks this way, without ever knowing it.

Suddenly the man notices the streamlined shadow. He doesn't panic. Instead, the diver doesn't take his eyes off the shark.

If the shark becomes too curious, the man can get back to his boat by being very careful. The diver will never forget this face-to-face meeting.

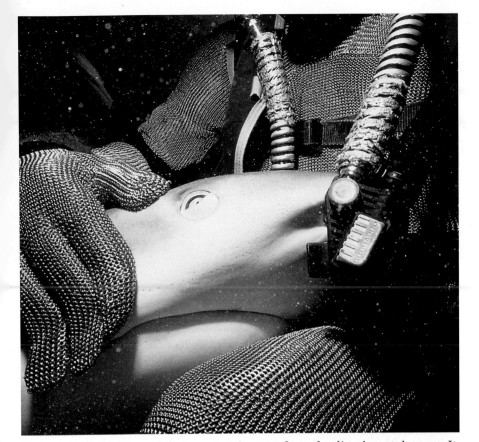

This shark closes its eyelids to protect its eyes from the diver's metal armor. It will pull away quickly once it has eaten the fish that attracted it.

Divers attract sharks with bait. By observing them in their habitat, the divers learn to respect them.

The Beast

Some people say that the shark is blood-thirsty and terrifying. Actually, it is fascinating. This magnificent marine predator is a perfect hunter whose form hasn't changed in millions of years. Today it is in danger of extinction from commercial fishing and human pollution. Its future is uncertain.

Shark fins are a delicacy, popular in Asian markets. More than 60 countries export them to Asia and the demand keeps growing.

A Bad Reputation

Sharks inspire fear. But only five species are ever a danger to humans: the blue shark, the great white, the oceanic whitetip, the bull shark, and the tiger shark. They've ruined the reputation of all the others.

While bees and snakes kill thousands of victims every year, only twenty to thirty people are killed each year by sharks. In that same time, humans kill 100 million sharks. Who is the true predator, man or shark?

Fishing or Massacre?

Every part of a shark can be used: the meat, the oil from its liver, the leather from its skin—and for medical purposes, the anticoagulants from its blood, the cornea from its eyes, and its cartilage.

But this unloved animal is killed carelessly. Perhaps half of the sharks caught each year are thrown back into the sea after the shark's fins are cut off. We waste food while the number of sharks drops dramatically.

22

Studying Sharks

Researchers now know that sharks are shy and never attack without a reason. Some sharks can dive twenty times deeper than dolphins. They are naturally resistant to cancer and may help us find a cure.

To study sharks, researchers place loudspeakers under water that emit low-frequency sounds. These sound like a struggling fish, and never fail to attract sharks quickly.

Shark Tips

When confronted with a shark, always remain facing it, don't lose your cool, don't make sudden movements, and don't cry out—panic triggers the attack.

"Monsters" in Danger

What are sharks good for? Who worries about their future? Many still think that the only good shark is a dead shark.

But sharks play an essential role at the top of the food chain. As predators, they feed on weak, injured, or sick animals. Their disappearance would endanger the fragile balance of the oceans. Many species are being driven to extinction. Will we live to see a world without sharks? Their survival depends on the respect and tolerance of humans.

Drift nets are deadly to sharks who have to swim to keep water flowing over their gills. Caught in the trap, they die of lack of oxygen.

23

Other Sharks

Sharks belong to the class Chondrichthyes, like rays, skates, and chimaeras. There are over 400 species of sharks. Almost every year, new species are discovered. Sharks can look very different: from the whale shark, the world's largest fish, to a shark that would fit in the palm of your hand. All of them have a cartilage skeleton, a skin covered with denticles, and an upper jaw which can open like the lower one.

▲ The *Blacktipped Reef Shark* is common around islands and in lagoons. It grows up to six feet long. Able to swim in only inches of water, it often approaches the edge of beaches. Careful! It feeds on fish and squid, but can attack swimmers' legs. . . .

◄ The *Great White Shark* reaches over twenty feet and can weigh more than two tons. This is the shark of nightmares. But it isn't really a "man-eater." Used to attacking seals and tortoises, it sometimes mistakenly bites swimmers who, seen from below, resemble its prey. Of course, the truth doesn't mean they aren't frightening, even with the protection of a cage.

The *Hammerhead Shark* is the ▶
most unusual-looking shark. It
may use its oddly shaped head
like a rudder to help it to turn
rapidly. It can catch extremely
agile prey, such as squid, on the
fly. Among the nine species of
hammerhead, the largest grow
up to twenty feet long.

▲
The *Wobbegong Shark* is the king of
camouflage. The spots that cover it mean it
is easily confused with the rocky bottom.
When an octopus, a crab or a fish passes
within range, it pounces to catch it with its
hooked teeth.

The *Sawshark* doesn't grow to more than ▶
four feet. It is found as deep as 3,000 feet.
It uses its long snout to batter and shred
its prey. To avoid hurting the mother
during birth, the baby sawshark is born
with a flexible saw which hardens
over time.

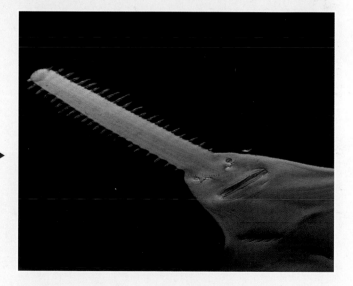

◀ There are many species of *Dogfish*. This one measures only two feet in length. It stays close to the bottom and feeds on mollusks and crustaceans. This habit means it is easily caught by trawlers and it is often found at fish markets. The dogfish family lives worldwide. In 1996, scientists discovered thirteen new shark species in New Caledonia. Eight belonged to the dogfish family.

The *Port Jackson Shark,* a type of bullhead shark, may grow to be three feet long, but it doesn't make a good meal: the long spines hidden in its fins get caught in the throat of its predators. Its blunt snout shelters broad flat teeth which it uses to crush its daily menu: sea urchins, crabs, starfish and even small fish. ▶

The *Whale Shark*, up to ▶ sixty feet long and weighing over forty tons, is the largest fish in the world. Fortunately, its gaping jaws with thousands of teeth only filter plankton and small fish. This enormous, peaceful fish occasionally accepts gentle pats and even tolerates being ridden.

▲ The *Oceanic Whitetip Shark*, which can grow to over twelve feet, is the most dangerous shark. Every day it covers considerable distances. Fortunately it only lives in the open ocean, where the water is at least 5,000 feet deep.

The *Sand Tiger Shark* can reach up to ▶ ten feet. It looks terrifying, but is completely harmless, because it can only catch small fish and squid. People kill it anyway, just because it looks frightening.

For Further Reading on Sharks . . .

Berman, Ruth. <u>Sharks</u>. Carolrhoda Books, 1995.

Cerullo, Mary M. <u>Coral Reef: A City That Never Sleeps</u>. Cobblehill Books (Dutton), 1996.

McGovern, Ann. <u>Questions and Answers about Sharks</u>. Scholastic, 1995.

Simon, Seymour. <u>Sharks</u>. HarperCollins, 1995.

To See Sharks in Captivity . . .

Batten, Mary. <u>Shark Attack Almanac</u>. Kidbacks, Random House, 1997.

Folzenlogen, Darcy and Robert. <u>The Guide to American Zoos and Aquariums</u>. Willow Press, 1993.

Many aquariums also have web sites on the internet. To learn more about their exhibits, go to the following page on the Yahoo WWW site:

http://dir.yahoo.com/Science/Biology/Zoology/Zoos/Aquariums

Use the Internet to Find Out More About Sharks . . .

Fiona's Shark Mania
http://www.oceanstar.com/shark

Kid's Web
http://www.npac.syr.edu/textbook/kidsweb/biology.html

Shark information from the Mote Marine Laboratory
http://www.mote.org/~rhueter/sharks/shark.phtml

The National Aquarium in Baltimore
http://www.aqua.org/animals/species/sharks.html

See Updated Animal Close-Ups Internet Resources . . .
http://www.charlesbridge.com

Photograph Credits

Cover: © Bill Curtsinger

BIOS Agency:
Y. Lefevre: pp. 4 (top), 6-7, 9 (bottom left), 9 (top), 10-11, 12-13, 15, 16, 25 (top right and bottom); J.-C. Robert: pp. 4, 6 (bottom), 8, 17 (bottom), 20 (bottom), 21 (bottom); H. Auslos: pp. 3, 9 (bottom); L. Funkhouser/P. Arnold: p. 12 (middle); H. Caroll/P. Arnold; p. 14 (bottom left); K. Aitken/P. Arnold: pp. 17 (top), 27 (bottom); J.-L. Rotman/P. Arnold: pp. 19 (middle), 21 (top), 24 (bottom); Y. Tavernier: pp. 19 (bottom), 20 (top); R. Seitre: p. 20 (middle); F. Bavedam: pp. 23 (bottom), 25 (top left), 26 (bottom), 27 (top right); G. Martin: p. 24 (top); D. Heuclin: p. 26 (top)

R. le Bloas and J. Julienne: pp. 4-5, 22; P. Deynat: p. 7 (bottom right); W.R. Strong: pp. 12 (top and botom), 23 (top); D. Doubilet: pp. 18-19, 19 (top).

With sincere thanks to Bernard Seret of ORSTOM for his scientific advice.